WEAR
THE
SKIRT

A RETURN TO WOMANHOOD

TOYA EXNICIOUS

THIS BOOK IS DEDICATED TO
my mother, Daphne Johnson,
and my father, Rinaldo Johnson.

They were the first to believe
in me and my many gifts.

Rest in peace, Pop!

INTRODUCTION

If you saw my bookshelf at home, you'd notice I have journals on top of journals. Some date back as far as 16 years and counting. Journaling has been my way to reflect and escape for many years. My friends laugh at me because I skim through books instead of reading them. Or, I pick up a book, read the table of contents and somehow I'm the expert on that book. I knew if I was going to write a book, it had to be true to me and it couldn't be in a format I don't read. So I decided to do a journal with snapshot thoughts.

I have a special, tender place in my heart for women and all of the issues we face daily. We are the glue holding many worlds together. It is not an easy job. I've worn many hats in my life. Sometimes I wonder how I made it. One thing has always worked for me: taking things one day and step at a time. Every page and quote represents a single step and a single thought. It's my desire you take each thought meditate and apply what you've learned. Journal it. This is an interactive book. It's not necessarily meant to be read front to back at a particular pace. It's meant to be experienced. Take in the words and sit for a quiet moment before moving on to the next thought.

I pray your life will be touched and you become a better woman, wife, sister and friend. This is what womanhood is all about. It's about YOU first. You're a woman first before you are a wife, mother, student, CEO, pastor, friend, etc. Every other role was assumed over time.

The first step in returning to womanhood is taking ownership of your own journey: your strengths, weaknesses, triumphs, and failures. Make an investment of time and energy into the woman you are and everything you hope to become. The world cannot get better around you, until it first gets better within you. Thank you for investing in this book. **Happy journaling!**

RELATIONSHIP

QUOTES & CHALLENGES

LOVE. LOVE. LOVE. LOVE. LOVE.

Focusing on love puts the world in perspective:
<u>God's love for us, love for ourselves, love for others.</u>
The same energy that we give to worry, doubt, un-forgiveness,
and fear can be replaced with energy given to love.

Love is not something you obtain,
it's something you become.

Think on the one thing that's weighing most
on your mind, that you're concerned about.

ASK YOURSELF
"WHAT AM I AFRAID OF".

Then reconcile the idea that <u>God (who is love)</u>
<u>is with you, will never fail you</u>, and has already
prepared you for all possible outcomes. And the outcome
that a loving Father establishes for His children is....

WE ALWAYS WIN!!!

CHALLENGE #1

WEAR THE "WHATEVER"

Just for today, tune out all that is wrong with the world around you
and dial into your resolve to see good and do good. This is not an
invitation to bury your head in the sand and pretend like nothing's
wrong. Rather, it is an invitation to allow people to be who they
are and do what they do while you focus on doing what you are
called to do today.

I DON'T
HOLD
GRUDGES

I LEARN
LESSONS

CHALLENGE #2

WEAR THE LESSON

You've been hurt by the people around you. Single out one of those situations today and write down what it has taught you about life and how it can serve as a reminder to do better in the future.

NOBODY WANTS TO BE CONSTANTLY BE REMINDED
OF HOW TERRIBLE THEY ARE.

In most cases, as individuals we stay on top of that job pretty adequately ourselves. We harbor so much insecurity, inadequacy, and inferiority within our own self-conscious just based on our life experiences alone. Let's all just stop being one another's negative conscious.

STOP BELITTLING PEOPLE.
STOP pointing out everyone's flaws and reminding them of their mistakes.

When people leave your presence they should feel like a winner, a champion.....not accused, guilty and unworthy. Loving the loveable is easy, but loving the unlovable is something we all have to work diligently at. I just know, in my most unlovable and perceived unforgiveable moments I would like nothing more than for someone to simply

SHOW ME LOVE.

CHALLENGE #3

WEAR THE LOVE

Intentionally love someone who has recently hurt you. Name one thing you can do for them today (a phone call, a text, a small gift, a lunch date, a compliment) that will let them know that you love them BEYOND their less-than-perfect actions.

"If you love me, you wouldn't hurt me".

ON WHAT PLANET?!?!?

People who love you, WILL hurt you.
Sometimes intentionally, other times not.
And there are times when people who
genuinely love you will hurt you the most.

People will fail you. They will disappoint you.

It's a fact of life.

And even with all of that said,
it's still OUR responsibility to love those who hurt us
and forgive people who have mistreated us.

WE STILL HAVE TO LEARN TO
LET GO &
MOVE FORWARD.

CHALLENGE #4

WEAR THE FORGIVENESS

People will hurt you. It's just the way that we work as human
beings. We hurt each other. Sometimes it's for reasons we don't
understand. But if we want long-lasting relationships, we're going
to have to learn to forgive. Today's challenge is to think of a specific
person you need to forgive for hurting you. AND THEN DO IT.
That forgiveness may be a decision in your mind, or it may be an
action you need to take or words you need to say. Whatever it is,
forgive them and decide to move on.

....

....

....

....

....

....

....

....

....

....

....

....

....

....

....

....

....

....

....

....

....

....

....

♡

Instead of wiping away tears,
START WIPING AWAY
THE
PEOPLE
THAT
CAUSE
THEM.

CHALLENGE #5

WEAR THE ELIMINATION

It's time to take some serious inventory of your relationships. Which ones bring you joy and laughter? Which ones bring you pain? Relationships have been designed by God in part to fulfill us, not to leave us hurt, broken, and confused. Which unproductive relationships in your life need to go? Let them.

Sometimes we have this idealistic view of
love & relationships.
The perfect partnership where sparks fly & stars align.
Could be because I'm a woman, but I feel
women are more guilty of this than men.
We want the ring, the wedding,
the perfect gentleman, two kids & a dog.
And we think all of this is gonna happen at no cost to us.
Love ain't easy & it ain't pretty.

It's grimy, dirty, dingy, strong, powerful, intense...

and it comes at the cost of being challenged & pushed
toward change. Sometimes you find a great man, but
because he challenges you, you run. Or get offended.
Or build walls to protect yourself. I know. I've done it.

**Is it possible that the biggest divide between you
& the love you seek is your unwillingness
to bend, concede, be challenged, and change.**

JUST MAYBE...

CHALLENGE #6

WEAR THE PERSPECTIVE

What wrong expectations do you have of the people you are in
relationship with? How are those expectations hindering your
relationships from moving forward and keeping you from growing?

....

....

....

....

....

....

....

....

....

....

....

....

....

....

....

....

....

....

....

....

....

....

....

....

.... ♡

My beautiful sisters & friends:

**STOP REMOVING YOUR CROWNS,
STEPPING OFF YOUR THRONES,
AND TARNISHING YOUR HALOS.**

You're worthy of true love.

Sacrificial love. Loyalty. Protection.
Genuine interest. Exclusivity. Affection. Pursuit.
Stop talking your way into counterfeits.
Convincing yourself that it's the real thing.
Believing that, that's the best you can get.
Sure, no man is perfect, but he should be intentional.....

ABOUT LOVING YOU!

The process of believing you're worth
true & full love is, indeed, a process.
I still struggle with that. Maybe in some way we all do.
I think you believe as you go. *Sometimes by faith.*
And sometimes God is just faithful enough to be
more love than you're even able to believe for.

CHALLENGE #7

WEAR THE WORTHINESS

In what relationships have you allowed yourself to settle for less
than God's best? Why? Is it because you believe that you aren't
worthy of it or will never get it? If so, why do you believe that?
Where did it come from? And what steps can you take to correct
that wrong thinking?

YOU CAN'T RESPOND TO EVERYTHING.

Some things, conversations, attitudes, and opinions just don't deserve your attention.

CHALLENGE #8

WEAR THE FOCUS

What is one thing that someone else has said or done to you or about you that has distracted you from what's really important? Forget about that for today. Keep your focus forward. What you give attention to will be magnified in your life. Make sure you make the important things big and the trivial things small.

SO, LADIES.......

you definitely need a man to treat you right,

BUT NO ONE REALLY OWES YOU ANYTHING.

How is it that YOU get to make a list of the
50 things you want in a man without ever considering
just how SHORT your own list is coming up?
Listen to all the relationship gurus if you want....
telling you how a man needs to be
worthy of YOUR love;
but then report back here when he moves on
after figuring out you aren't "worthy" of his.

CHALLENGE #9

WEAR THE LIST

But not this list of things you want in a man or deserve from the one
you have. Instead, make a list of ways you can mirror or give that
back to someone in your life.

....
....
....
....
....
....
....
....
....
....
....
....
....
....
....
....
....
....
....
....
....
....
....
....
....
....
....
....

♡

I don't claim to know everything about love and relationships, but there are a few things that I understand now, that I didn't once upon a time. Have you ever noticed that some of the most beautiful women are often single and/or bouncing from relationship to relationship? **Well, that's because beauty, big butts, a pretty face, and good sex aren't enough to sustain a successful relationship**. A woman will not be successful in a relationship with a man until she becomes relevant to his work & a necessary, vital part of his success and achievement. As women, we are socialized toward the fairytale. Men are socialized toward accomplishment. Your pretty face, nice body, and financial demands will only be seen as a burden to a man who is busy about success and achievement. If your presence in his life is not a representation of peace and help, it will be more of a headache to keep you around than a benefit. I understand you have your list of the 50 things you desire in a man & that's ok. **AT THE SAME TIME, START WORKING ON YOUR LIST OF THE TOP 10 ELEMENTS OF VALUE THAT YOU POSSESS THAT CAN BE OF BENEFIT TO THE TYPE OF MAN YOU DESIRE.**

CHALLENGE #10

WEAR THE TABLE

As in what are you bringing to it? Relationships cannot be one-sided. What are you bringing to the table in a relationship? How does that enhance a man's life and help him accomplish his goals?

QUOTES & CHALLENGES

I hate clichés, but the age old
"beauty is skin deep" is true.
Seems like every woman
is caged by a set of lies
that came from somewhere.

You're too skinny...you're too fat.....your stomach isn't flat....at 5'3" you should weigh 125 lbs.....your legs aren't thick...you don't have a butt....etc., etc., etc.

So we live our lives in these prisons of lies,

SCARED, SCARRED & BOUND!
I just wanna take the key & let everybody out.

DEFINE IT FOR YOURSELF & WALK IN IT!!!!

CHALLENGE #11

WEAR THE DEFINITION

What is sexy to you? What does it mean for you? For your life? For the way that you dress? Are you in a box when it comes to seeing your own sexiness? Break out of it! Define sexy for yourself and list one way you're going to walk in that today.

You confront your honest, true self
& at first it's ugly.
You wanna turn away from the bitter,
naked truth about yourself. YOU WANNA RUN.
It's easier that way. You run from the imperfect you
& in like manner consistently run from everything
that's imperfect around you.
**It's a pattern, a habit. But one day you're gonna see the
imperfect you & sit with it. You're gonna park there**

After you accept your own flaws & imperfect situations,
you'll begin to love and accept those who are also
imperfect around you & realize everything is gonna
turn out just fine with them too.

CHALLENGE #12

WEAR THE IMPERFECTION

Nobody's perfect. You may feel you're overweight. Maybe you've got oily skin or acne scars. Whatever it is, embrace that imperfection. Because nothing you do with your wardrobe is ever going to be authentic or true if you don't first love the person wearing the clothes.

this is one of those **"if the shoe fits"** type of messages. Don't shoot the messenger. Just sit with it for five minutes before you write me off as crazy... if it challenges you, good...**IT SHOULD**: Married women, I would recommend you take one evening to go out into an environment where there are a lot of single women. **Just <u>ONE</u> night.** Take inventory of the way they present themselves. **The amount of thought that obviously went into every detail of the way they present themselves (hair, nails, makeup, oils, perfumes, lotion, dresses, skirts, etc...).** Then pause and think about yourself...

You can make a change, or make excuses. But this may be why he's looking at you with the *side eye* when he get home. *Let that sink in for a second.*

CHALLENGE #13

WEAR THE REALITY CHECK

Have you let yourself go? How much thought are you truly putting into your appearance every day? This isn't just about married women. This is about all women. News flash: your appearance matters. If this applies to you, take some time to think about why you have devalued your outward beauty. Then, list one thing you're going to do today to re-invest in it.

Whoever said that

HAIR, NAILS, MAKEUP, AND CLOTHES

are superficial, has obviously never seen
a woman fresh out the

NAIL/HAIR SALON, NEW THREADS, AND A SNATCHED FACE!

#TheGraceOfBeauty

CHALLENGE #14

WEAR THE FRESH LOOK

Today's challenge is simple: Do your hair. Paint your nails. Go buy a new outfit or wear the clothes you have in a combo you've never put together before. Break some makeup rules and try a bold new lipstick and eyeshadow combination. And watch how many selfies you're inclined to take today.

A lot of people have great things to say, positive messages, but the way they physically present themselves makes me not want to listen.

People's first impression of you is the way you dress & carry yourself.
WHY WOULD I LISTEN TO YOUR WORDS FOR ENCOURAGEMENT IF YOUR APPEARANCE LOOKS DOWN TRODDEN, SAD, AND DEPRESSING?!?!?
Welp.....somebody had to say it!
Let the chips fall where they may...

CHALLENGE #15

WEAR THE IMPRESSION

Ask 10 people you come across today what impression they get just from looking at you. Write down what they say. Is it positive? Was it what you wanted to hear? What do you need to change so that your appearance makes the impression that you want it to make?

Ladies, surround yourself with other women you aspire to be like. Yes, we think about that in terms of finances, success, family, and other things, but you already know that isn't what I'm talking about.

Hang around a bunch of raggedy females, that's how you're going to be.

*I KEEP BAD CHICKS AROUND ME. IT KEEPS ME ON TOP OF MY GAME.

CHALLENGE #16

WEAR THE STYLIST

Call a friend you consider to have top-notch style and wears stuff that you could never pull off. Let her be your stylist for the day. See what happens.

"Listen — read the covers of magazines
and you'd think romance is a function of
cleavage and plastic surgeon noses and spray tans.
Read the glossy covers and you'd think
love is a function of waist size and heel height
and bare flesh flaunted for every gawking eye.

That's what the media is selling: X-rated Beauty.
Romance Porn. That's the thing about the check-out line:
<u>The media's fueled by changing the definition of beauty,
romance, and love from what is true to what is trendy.</u>
Media tries to define you with likes as a measure of your
love-ability. Media votes you on or votes you off,
as if a woman's worth is a popularity contest
instead of being permanently won by function of

BEING MADE IN THE IMAGE AND LIKENESS OF GOD."

*- from Dear Women & Daughters: When You're Tired of
Media Voices Telling You What Beauty & Love Is*

CHALLENGE #17

WEAR THE WORD

Forget the media for today. God has something to say about your
worth and your beauty. Find one scripture where His words are
affirming your beauty. Write it down on a card. Take it with you
and confess it today.

Don't compare yourself to other people.

PERIOD.

Yes, get better, but get better at being you.
Don't spend time getting better because you
feel inadequate in comparison to someone else.
Aren't you glad Steve Jobs didn't try to be Bill Gates?
The world was able to benefit from both gifts.

THE WORLD NEEDS YOU!
THE AUTHENTIC YOU!

Not a partial you, or you trying to act like somebody else.

CHALLENGE #18

WEAR THE COMPLIMENT

We women are not competing against each other. When we learn to compliment another woman on the way she looks, we acknowledge that there's room here for the both of us to walk in the full expression of our beauty. Compliment a random woman on her makeup, hair, or outfit today. Take note of how secure and powerful it makes you feel to have the confidence to acknowledge another's beauty knowing that it doesn't diminish your own.

The great thing about art is that there are no rules.

It's why religious minds attack it.
They want rules and boxes.

SEES A
BLANK SPACE & IT

CAGED MINDS CAN'T CREATE.

CHALLENGE #19

WEAR THE CREATIVITY

Let your creativity run free today in the way that you dress, style your hair, and do your makeup. Think of yourself as a work of art, something to be beheld. Carefully curate your look today, selecting patterns, colors, and styles that will make you look like moving art. Don't stop to think about what others might think. Just see where your creativity takes you.

I swear I wanna push all kinds of
LIMITS & BOUNDARIES.
And not even the world's limits.
Not even society's limits.
I wanna push the boundaries & limitations
IN MY OWN MIND.

what I've told MYSELF is or isn't possible.
I wanna question my own "absolutes" & "norms"
to see what sticks.
At this point, I'm beyond (caring OR wondering)
if people accept me. But I've decided that
THERE'S NO WAY
you will encounter me & NOT feel SOMETHING!

CHALLENGE #20

WEAR THE SURPRISE

Wear something today that's totally out of your comfort zone. Maybe it's a skirt or shorts that show off those legs you don't like. Maybe it's a tank top that reveals those arms that have a stretch mark or two. Maybe it's a V-neck cut just a little lower than you would normally have it. Whatever it is, get out of the box. Surprise the people around you. Push yourself to the limit with your choices and own that expanded territory without apology today.

LIFE

QUOTES & CHALLENGES

BEGIN.
AGAIN.
IT'S NEVER TOO LATE
to get up
&
try again.

CHALLENGE #21

WEAR THE DO-OVER

We try things. We fail. And the fear of failing again stops us from ever trying again. The first step to making real, lasting change is getting rid of that fear and being willing to try again. What failed dream are you afraid of pursuing again? Today, get up, dust yourself off, and take a tiny step towards it. What is that step?

In my lifetime I've sought after many things.
**I've dreamt of big houses, nice cars, diamonds,
the killer wardrobe, designer bags & shoes.**
I set my sights & worked hard
with this end result in mind.
And while all those things are nice & quality things
are something every human deserves to have;

IT'S JUST NOT THAT IMPORTANT
TO ME ANYMORE.

Nowadays, I work hard so my mother won't have to.
<u>I work so that I can build a legacy</u>
<u>for my family and future children.</u>
I now cherish time spent more than money spent.
I value connection & priceless moments
more than doing the most
just for the sake of doing the most.
Maybe I'm getting old.

OR MAYBE I'M JUST NOW REALIZING
WHAT LIFE IS REALLY ABOUT.

CHALLENGE #22

WEAR THE "WHY"

We all have a dream. But the passion to see that dream through to fruition is going to be fueled by our "why". And that "why" has to be bigger than money. Why do you do what you do? Why are you pursuing the goal you're after? Write it down, make it plain. Take it to heart. And let it fuel your drive for success today.

Safe. Easy. Comfortable.
Status Quo.
I'M UNINTERESTED.
And it shouldn't interest you either.
If your dreams and visions don't scare you,

THEY'RE
NOT BIG
ENOUGH.

When was the last time you put it all on line?
Do u even know what that feels like?
At some point in your lifetime, you should.

CHALLENGE #23

WEAR THE WILDEST DREAM

If you close your eyes and imagine your life on the grandest scale, what does it look like? Where are you and what are you doing? Are you making impact across the nations? Are you speaking to executive officials about your policy ideas? Are your fashion lines walking down the most well-known runways all over the world? Dare to dream today, and write down what that dream is and what it looks like. Don't be tempted to water it down because it feels silly or unachievable.

MY #1 LIFE MANTRA

THERE'S ALWAYS AT LEAST 3 WAYS
TO DO ANY ONE THING.

Don't marry methods.

STAY COMMITTED
TO YOUR DECISIONS;
BUT REMAIN FLEXIBLE
IN YOUR APPROACH.

CHALLENGE #24

WEAR THE STRATEGY

Do this. Think of 3 ways you can achieve the dream or goal you've set for your life. Really strategize three paths that could lead you to where you want to be.

FAITH
DOESN'T
CONSIDER
INTELLECT.

CHALLENGE #25

WEAR THE POSITIVE THOUGHT

We're good at listing over and over again all the reasons why it won't work. Today, list in your journal all of the reasons why it will.

THERE'S A DIFFERENCE BETWEEN A GIFT & A CALLING.

CHALLENGE #26

WEAR THE INVENTORY

Your calling is that thing you're supposed to be doing. Your gifts are what's going to facilitate the calling. What has God put in your heart to do? What gifts do you have that will facilitate that calling? Take inventory of them and write them down.

One body. Many parts.

If you're an eye....can you really tell the nose
how to smell, the ear how to hear, the hand how to feel?

NO, YOU CAN'T.

It's crazy to think that as an eye you can set up a meeting
with a finger and say, "you know, you aren't touching that
the right way". Sounds crazy, right?
If you're an eye...focus on being an eye.
The whole body needs you to do your job: SEE.
The finger needs you to focus on seeing, because when
you do, it helps them know what to grab, touch, feel.
Stop jumping out of the socket and focusing on the job
of the other parts of the body. Keep seeing. The nose will
keep smelling. The mouth will keep speaking.
The ear will keep hearing. The hand will keep touching.

TRANSLATION:

Stay in your lane. Perfect YOUR CRAFT and YOUR ROLE.

You are not an expert on ALL THINGS, but when we all
do OUR PART at the highest level of efficiency....

THE BODY LIVES.

CHALLENGE #27

WEAR THE LANE

It's time for some real self-reflection. Are there people whose
gifts, calling, titles, etc. you wish you had? Why? What do you
think is better about their callings or gifts? What is it about your
calling and gift that you can appreciate? Where do you fit in the
body? What are YOU doing to help it function as it's supposed to?

I have intentionally surrounded myself with visionaries.
I intentionally only spend my time
focused on forward progress.
I wanna talk about how can we charter flights to the
moon. How we can create our own political parties.
Ways to change legislation. Music. Art. Travel. God.

THE AFTERLIFE.

I don't like taking about "one day someone is going to
come along and change the world", or "if only someone
would do something about this or that".
I prefer to surround myself with minds who know that
WE are it! WE are the world changers.
WE DON'T TALK ABOUT MOVEMENTS.
WE DON'T WAIT FOR MOVEMENTS.

WE ARE THE
MOVEMENT.

CHALLENGE #28

WEAR THE CIRCLE

As in "Who's in yours"? Take a moment to think about who you have surrounded yourself with. Are they people helping to push you forward as they move forward in their particular calling? Or are they standing still? You are who you hang with. Evaluate your circle today. Name at least 3 people who are on the path with you and intentionally resolve to strengthen those friendships and relationships.

Things u see were not made from things u see.
Things u see were created by things u can't see.

**The fruit of your life is based on
the things u think, say, and believe.**
STOP TRYING TO CHANGE
PHYSICAL
THINGS
WITH
PHYSICAL
THINGS.

CHALLENGE #29

WEAR THE CONFESSION

Our beliefs shape our lives. Our words shape our beliefs. The way to change your life is to change the words you speak. Today, write out a confession for your life. Include affirmations of your vision and speak it into existence. Commit to making this confession daily and take notice of how it impacts your thoughts, beliefs, and behaviors.

In 2001 my sister & I started a ministry for young adults. We'd rent cars to pick people up just to minister to them. We would rent hotel meeting spaces to minister to those same people. We did it out of our own pocket. In 2001 I started working (employed) in full time ministry. In 2003 I started working in youth ministry, speaking & ministering to youth & young adults. In 2006 I started a mentorship program for teen girls, that eventually led to conferences with multiplied hundreds of girls. In 2010 I started **TPrissy Worldwide** while working a full time job. In 2013 I left my full time job in order to devote more time to TPrissy Worldwide events and did 100% of them free of charge. January 2015 was my first paid event. That's FOURTEEN YEARS of consistent work before I legitimately had my own and made any level of profit. And I'm STILL just getting started. <u>Moral: don't say you want to do anything if you're not willing to consistently put in work.</u> Don't try to mimic what someone else is doing, if you're not AT LEAST willing to mimic their work ethic. Don't assume anything about a person until you know the WHOLE STORY. NOTHING JUST HAPPENS. THERE'S NO SUCH THING AS OVERNIGHT SUCCESS. True success is established little-by-little. You will not be entrusted with your own until you are faithful over that which is another man's. Stop giving up so easy. You have to go through the process & stay the course.

CHALLENGE #30

WEAR THE WORK

This has become a dirty word in Christian circles. Yes, grace is available to us, but it's there to help us as we do the WORK we've been assigned. Go back to the first quote in this section and let your why fuel your work today. And then list one thing you're going to do every day for the NEXT 30 days to WORK toward your dreams.

CPSIA information can be obtained
at www.ICGtesting.com
Printed in the USA
LVHW072358190320
650657LV00010B/1291

* 9 7 8 1 5 3 0 4 6 0 8 9 2 *